Discover Yourself

MARTIN FORMATO

Copyright © 2014 Martin Formato

All rights reserved.

ISBN-10: 1523873477
ISBN-13: 978-1523873470

Disclaimer

The information is of a general nature and does not take into account your personal situation. The information presented is for educational purposes only. The author will not bear any responsibility or liability for any action taken by any person, persons or organization on the purported basis of the information contained in this book and any supporting material. References to other information, websites or events should not be understood as an endorsement of such information, website or events. Every effort has been made to ensure that this book is free from errors or omissions. However, the author shall not accept responsibility for injury, loss or damage occasioned to any person acting or refraining from action as a result of material in this book whether or not such injury, loss or damage is in any way due to any negligent act or omission, breach of duty or default on the part of the author.

DEDICATION

I dedicate this book to my father for giving me a kick when I needed it; and my mother for catching me when I was falling.

CONTENTS

1 INTRODUCTION

I want to thank you and congratulate you for buying this book, "Discover Yourself".

Hi, I am Martin Formato, a professional certified life and business coach, motivational speaker and author of the self-help book, "**Follow Your Own Path**".

This book is about the most important person in the world, YOU.

This book contains proven steps and strategies on how to discover yourself and find out who you really are.

The first step of this life enhancing process is about self discovery. It's about looking at your past and present situation.

You get a better understanding of yourself by taking a close look at where you came from; what your experiences have been; what you believe in; who you are today; where you are at in the various areas of your life; what you are capable of; what you can improve; what resources or help you have access to and what makes you happy.

Surprisingly enough, most people don't know or have forgotten who they are.

This step can be broken down into the following areas:

Who Am I Today?
Find My Superpowers

My Past
My Beliefs
Life Phases
Wheel of Life
My Strengths
Which Areas Can I Improve?
What Resources or Help Do I Have Access To?
What Makes Me Happy?
6 Core Human Needs
My Values

Inside this book you will find proven processes that, if you follow, will allow you to discover yourself.

This book all started with the idea that if I can help just one person to learn one thing that will help make their life better, then the time I have spent writing this book will have been totally worth it. And it has done just that many times over.

There is nothing in this book that will be difficult for you.

All you have to do is read, think, write and take action.

Writing is important because, as you put your thoughts on paper, it clears your mind allowing it to function more efficiently. By putting your thoughts on paper, you will be able to group, analyze and process actions on them or discard them. This allows you to step out of yourself and look at yourself from a different perspective, to take a helicopter view of your life.

"**Discover Yourself**" is a book that will give you insight information about yourself that you may not have considered before. You will learn how to look at yourself differently. There are many questions that I will ask you in this book, the reason being that you are best placed to answer these. You are the expert in your life, not me.

By the end of this book you will know yourself better. You will know your strengths and what makes you happy. This information is very important. It is your foundation. It will help you decide which direction to take in life so you can achieve peace, success and happiness.

Here is to you and your quest to create a life you love!

One of my objectives is to ensure that you enjoy this book. So if you have any questions, comments or suggestions for improvement, please email me at martin@martinformato.com

2 WHO AM I TODAY?

"We act, behave and feel according to what we consider our self-image to be and do not deviate from that pattern."

Maltz

Stop and look in the mirror.

You know yourself better than anyone else does.

Who you are today really depends upon where you are, whom you're with and what you're doing. Different influences cause us to have different moods and, consequently, behave in different ways.

To make the process of identifying who you are easier, think carefully about who you are when in your positive environments as well as your negative ones. You might not like some things that you see but remember that there are things you can change if you really want to.

Where you are as a person today and the person you aspire to be can be two different things. In recognising your personality traits, your strengths, areas you can improve, what resources and help you have access to, you are actively noting the personal changes you must make to become the person you aspire to be. Realizing exactly who you are today will assist you in realising who you want to be in the future.

At the moment, most of us have a list of things that we want to change. Big or small, we all want to make changes to become more content with our lives and ourselves.

Some of us feel that these changes are achievable whereas others feel they are not.

Having the confidence to believe that the changes are achievable is a major factor for making the changes happen. Putting a plan in place to effect the change and adhering to the plan is a sure bet that a change is on the way.

Who am I today?

How would you describe yourself to someone else?

For example: I am single and a technical support person working for a finance company. I am studying computer programming part time. I am easygoing, have a good sense of humour and like to socialise. I lead a very busy life.

Tips:

What do you spend most of your day doing?

What other roles do you play? For example, are you a husband, wife, father, mother etc?

How would you describe your personality? You may wish to try the following personality test at

http://bit.ly/2jWnVBy

Now, let's have a look at you. Write below, who you are:

3 FIND MY SUPERPOWERS

To be successful in whatever you do, you need to operate from your strengths, from your superpowers and not from your weaknesses.

Sometimes we're not aware of our superpowers which are right under our nose.

The best way to find these superpowers is to ask others. Others can see things that we don't.

Today's challenge is to email at least 9 people, that know you, and ask them what your superpowers are.

These people could be family members, friends, work colleagues, employees, the boss, clients or suppliers.

This is something that Pat Flynn and several other entrepreneurs have done because by knowing their superpowers they can take advantage of them. Once you know your superpowers then you too can take advantage of them.

Your superpowers can be a skill, an attribute, characteristic or talent that you have that no-one else has. These are your unfair advantage, your competitive edge that separates you from others. It's what makes you so special.

When I did this challenge, here is what people said:

Martin is

Positive
Enthusiastic
Empathetic
Caring
Considerate
Optimistic
Reliable
Efficient
Helpful
Cheeky (in a good way)
Focus, getting things done no matter what, analytical and logical problem solving
Self motivated, self analysis, thinking about where you want to be in the future, whilst still enjoying each day, and planning a set of goals, actions and determinations to journey and arrive at the desired destination
Persistence
Insistence
Alertness

I agree with what people have said. I am determined, self-motivated and I do my best to help people. Yes I also like to have fun in the process. I'm pleased that people have said these things about me because these qualities are required to be successful in the field of coaching, which is my passion.

Now it's your turn.

I've made it easy for you. Simply copy the text below in an email (with or without modification) and send it to at least 9 people that know you.

I suggest sending just one email to all of your contacts by adding their name in the BCC field in your email. They will not know who else you sent it to and only you will receive the reply. Substitute your name where it says [Your Name] and whichever applies where it says [he/she] or [him/her].

Subject: *From Martin Formato on behalf of [Your Name]*

Email:

Hi my name is Martin Formato and I'm a professional certified life coach who is helping [Your Name] find their superpowers. Don't worry; I'm not trying to sell you anything.

I've asked [Your Name] to send you this email because [he/she] needs your help and trusts that you'll give your honest opinion. This won't take more than a minute of your time.

I've challenged [Your Name] to discover a unique trait or skill that they are really good at – to find a sort of "superpower" that they possess that can be used to their advantage in life, at work or in business.

The best way to know this information is to hear it from others, that's why I've asked [Your Name] to email just a few select people.

If you could reply to this email with what you believe to be [Your Name's] "superpowers" or traits and characteristics that you believe to be unique, it would help out tremendously.

Only [Your Name] will see your reply and no-one else.

If you are not sure about this and want to make sure this is real you can email me at Martin@DoingWorkThatMatters.com or go to my website at www.DoingWorkThatMatters.com

I'm here to help [Your Name] and I'm thankful that you are too.

Cheers and all the best.
Martin Formato
Professional Certified Life & Workplace Coach
www.DoingWorkThatMatters.com

If you would like to send these out individually or change the message somewhat then you are free to do so.

The important thing is that you send it out, get a reply, so you can find out more about you... What makes you special?

When you receive your responses you may notice that there are some common themes. This is a good thing as it validates how you are being perceived by others.

I would love to read in the comments of my blog at http://martinformato.com/find-your-superpowers/ what people have said are your superpowers.

4 MY PAST

Everyone is influenced by experiences that occur every day in our lives. Obviously, the more profoundly affected by an experience we are, the bigger impact it has on shaping our personality and influencing our thoughts.

Learning more about who we are and how we think can be achieved by thinking carefully about significant events that have shaped us.

Consider the following questions and note down your answers.

What are the 3 events that you remember most in your life so far?

These can be good times or bad times.

For example:

When I broke my leg
My first kiss
Going on an overseas holiday
The birth of my child

Write your 3 memorable events here:

a)
b)
c)

What are the 3 experiences that you never want to have again?

For example:

Failing my school examination
Death of a family member
Losing my gold necklace
Feeling unfulfilled at work

Write yours here:

a)
b)
c)

During which 3 situations did you feel the weakest?

For example:

When I injured my back
When I had no money
When I was alone
When I had no job

Write yours here:

a)
b)
c)

During which 3 situations did you feel the strongest, the most in control of what you were doing?

For example:

When I got my first car
When I moved out of home
Whenever I am on holidays

Write yours here:

a)

b)
c)

What are the 3 experiences that you most want to relive?

For example:

My graduation ceremony
My 30th birthday
My world holiday

Write yours here:

a)
b)
c)

Think about these experiences and how they affect your thoughts, your feelings (emotions) and your behavior.

5 MY BELIEFS

When you believe something you feel certain about it. Beliefs are things we hold as being true or real, things in which we have faith or trust. Faith is a powerful tool. Believe in yourself, in what you do and who you are.

If your beliefs are positive then they help you. If they are negative or limiting then they hold you back. You are not born with these negative or limiting beliefs, someone put them there, meaning you can get rid of them.

It is best to change your negative or limiting beliefs to more positive or realistic ones. Positive beliefs are necessities for success.

We will look at how to change your negative or limiting beliefs to more positive or realistic beliefs later in this book. For now, just list your beliefs.

For example:

I am in control of my destiny
Life is difficult
I am here for a reason
How I treat others is how they will treat me
I have everything inside of me necessary to be great
There is no such thing as failure, only feedback
I am either part of the problem or part of the solution
You get what you deserve
No one can make me feel inferior without my consent
The world is not safe
If I hang around smart people I become smart
You can't buy love

I believe I have the capacity to make the changes I desire
I believe that you are the expert in your life
I believe that I have competencies and resources that I am not aware of

My beliefs are:

a)
b)
c)
d)
e)
f)
g)

6 LIFE PHASES

In life, we are usually in one of four life phases as defined below (from Frederic Hudson 1999 "The handbook of coaching" Jossey-Bass, San Francisco):

1. Feeling motivated and full of energy. Feeling confident, fulfilled and ready for any challenge.

2. Feeling bored in your job. Feeling a sense of decline, feeling stuck, and feeling trapped.

3. Feeling like you are in the middle of an identity crisis. Feeling lost and afraid with a sense that your life has no purpose. Feeling lonely and sad.

4. Starting to experiment with new ideas. Having a new sense of purpose, feeling creative, feeling comfortable in taking new risks.

Which life phase would you say you are in?

7 WHEEL OF LIFE

In today's busy world you may find your time and energy being spent in only a few areas of your life while other areas miss out. This makes it easy to get out of balance, leading to frustration and stress.

The wheel of life (created by Paul J. Meyer, founder of Success Motivation Institute, Inc.) can help you take a "helicopter view" of your life so you can see if any areas are out of balance.

This tool is used to measure your current level of satisfaction in various areas of your life. The 5 sections of the wheel (as a whole) represent the life-balance. The wheel helps you to determine if any areas of your life are out of balance and need attention.

Your life needs balance just like you need a balance of solid (food), liquid (water) and gas (air) to survive.

On a scale of 0 (being unsatisfied) to 10 (being very satisfied), how would you rate your current level of satisfaction in the following areas?

Spiritual (This is about your faith, values and beliefs)
Feeling at peace
Having purpose
Meaning of life
Serving others
Connection with others
Your faith
Living your values
Your belief

My Spiritual level of satisfaction rating is (0-10):

Mental (This is about your state of mind)
Intellectual
Knowledge
Learning
Career/business
Emotional
Frustration
Stress
Worry

My Mental level of satisfaction rating is (0-10):

Physical (This is about your physical health)
Exercise
Fitness
Flexibility
Strength
Nutrition
Water
Weight
Smoking
Alcohol
Drugs

My Physical level of satisfaction rating is (0-10):

Social (This is about your relationships)
Family
Friends
Community
Relationships

My Social level of satisfaction rating is (0-10):

Financial (This is about your finances)
Money
Debt
Assets
Liabilities
Income
Expenses
Shares
Property

My Financial level of satisfaction rating is (0-10):

Please note that your health, both mental and physical, is the most important area of your life as you can't achieve anything or help others if you are not well.

Once completed, your wheel of life can act as a guide to where more time and energy is required in order to achieve greater satisfaction in life.

For further insight into who you are today let's look closer at these 5 main areas of your life:

Spiritual
Mental
Physical
Social
Financial

Define your present status according to each of these 5 areas.

Spiritual

Your faith, values and beliefs.

Do you believe in a God or life after death?

For example: I believe that there is a God and that I should treat others how I expect to be treated.

What do you believe?

Mental

This is your state of mind.

Your Intellectual and Emotional status.

For example: <u>Intellectually</u>, I have the following qualifications or sought-after qualities:

Diploma in computer studies
Basic first aid training

What qualifications or sought-after qualities do you have?

For example: <u>Emotional</u> status, I am feeling (for example energetic, unfulfilled, stressed, satisfied, happy, bored, angry, trapped, anxious, unmotivated, tired, out of control): Unmotivated and tired.

How are you feeling emotionally right now?

Are you having fun never, sometimes, often or all the time?

Are you happy with your current level of fun? Yes or No

Do you need to have more fun? Yes or No

Physical

This is about your physical health. The condition of your body.

Are you under, of average or over weight?

Do you exercise regularly or occasionally?

Are you physically in good or poor health?

Do you look good, average, or not so good?

How do you feel physically?

Social

This is how you interact with other people. Your interpersonal relationships.

How would you describe your relationship with your family?

How would you describe your relationship with your friends?

How would you describe your relationship with your co-workers?

Financial

Your Net Financial Worth is the difference in value between what you **own** and what you **owe**.

For example:

MARTIN FORMATO

(What You Own)

(What You Owe)

Assets	Value
Cash	50
Bank Deposit	1,500
Motor Vehicles	
- Holden Astra	9,500
-	
Contents	
- Furniture	2,000
- Clothes	270
- TV/Radio	500
Family Home	635,000
Other Property	
- Holiday Home	
- Land/ Investment Property	
Shares	1,500
Superannuation	3,000
Bonds	
Others	
TOTAL Assets	**653,320**

Liabilities	Value
Bank Overdraft	
Credit Card	700
Loan	
- Personal	1,500
- Motor Vehicle	3,000
- Mortgage	245,000
Other Loans	
-	
-	
TOTAL Liabilities	**250,200**

TOTAL ASSETS	$	653,320
LESS TOTAL LIABILITIES	- $	250,200
EQUALS NET FINANCIAL WORTH	= $	403,120

What is my Net Financial Worth?

(What You Own)   (What You Owe)

Assets	Value		Liabilities	Value
Cash			Bank Overdraft	
Bank Deposit			Credit Card	
Motor Vehicles			Loan	
- Holden Astra			- Personal	
-			- Motor Vehicle	
Contents			- Mortgage	
- Furniture			Other Loans	
- Clothes			-	
- TV/Radio			-	
Family Home				
Other Property				
- Holiday Home				
- Land/ Investment Property				
Shares				
Superannuation				
Bonds				
Others				
TOTAL Assets			**TOTAL Liabilities**	

TOTAL ASSETS	$
LESS TOTAL LIABILITIES	- $
EQUALS NET FINANCIAL WORTH	= $

21

Your Net Annual Savings is the difference between the amount of **money coming in (income)** and the amount of **money going out (expenses)**.

(Money In)

Annual Income	Amount
Family Allowance/Pension	
Unemployment Benefits	
Bank Interest	75
Salary/Wages (after tax)	80,468
Bonuses	
Investment Rent	
Share Dividend	75
Others	
TOTAL Annual Income	**80,618**

(Money Out)

Annual Expenses	Amount
- Mortgage	26,000
- Rent	
- Telephone	600
- Electricity	350
- Gas	300
- Water	400
- Rates	420
- Maintenance	500
Food	27,800
Transport	1,200
- Petrol	2,200
- Service	500
Entertainment/Gifts	4,700
Health	800
Insurance – Car and House	800
TOTAL Annual Expenses	**66,570**

TOTAL Annual Income	$	80,618
TOTAL Annual Expenses	- $	66,570
EQUALS NET ANNUAL SAVINGS	= $	14,048

What are my Net Annual Savings?

(Money In)   (Money Out)

Annual Income	Amount
Family Allowance/Pension	
Unemployment Benefits	
Bank Interest	
Salary/Wages (after tax)	
Bonuses	
Investment Rent	
Share Dividend	
Others	
TOTAL Annual Income	

Annual Expenses	Amount
- Mortgage	
- Rent	
- Telephone	
- Electricity	
- Gas	
- Water	
- Rates	
- Maintenance	
Food	
Transport	
- Petrol	
- Service	
Entertainment/Gifts	
Health	
Insurance – Car and House	
TOTAL Annual Expenses	

TOTAL Annual Income	$
TOTAL Annual Expenses	- $
EQUALS NET ANNUAL SAVINGS	= $

Tip: Don't buy things you don't need, with money you don't have, to impress people you don't like.

What is your Net Financial Worth?

What are your Net Annual Savings?

Do you feel like you have or don't have control over your finances?

8 MY STRENGTHS

As human beings, we all have strengths and areas we can improve. It is important that we recognize what they are because it is these that shape our lives.

We need to use our strengths in ways that benefit us. At the same time, we need to develop areas we can improve into strengths.

Strengths help us to achieve our best. They are often also our talents and the characteristics for which we usually receive compliments. Capitalize on your strengths; they are your most valuable personal assets.

In competitions you should use your strengths, as they are your personal advantage over others. Your strengths are unique to you.

Think about and then list your **strengths** here:

For example:

I get things done quickly
I work well with people
I don't give up easily
I am a good cook
I have experience with computers
I have an easygoing nature
I am well organised
I am loyal and dependable
I am hospitable
I make decisions quickly

Tips:

What skill or special knowledge do you have?
Think of the strengths you have used to achieve past successes.
Most people find that the things they like doing are the same things they are good at, these are usually their strengths.
Ask your family and friends what they would say your strengths are.
Remember that strengths are the tools to help you achieve your goals.

My strengths are:

Following on from this, our strong points, or strengths, are often the contributing factors which make us successful.

We will be recognized for the confidence we exude when doing the things we enjoy doing, and also the natural talent that exudes whilst doing them.

To live a successful and fulfilling life we need to concentrate on spending as much of our day doing the things that we enjoy and expressing our natural talents.

Good qualities to have:

A capacity for self-observation and reflection
An ability to recognize what can be changed and what cannot
An ability to accept criticism and feedback
An awareness of your own personal fears
Setting high standards for yourself
A capacity to inspire others
Authenticity (practicing what you are teaching)
Self-discipline
Creativeness
Energy and enthusiasm

9 WHAT AREAS CAN I IMPROVE?

"There are two ways a person can grow in his or her mind. First, the person can seem to appear larger by making other people appear smaller. Secondly, the person can actually grow by concentrating upon and developing what he or she has and by helping others to do the same. The second method of growth leads to greater happiness and success in life."

Carl Mays

Weaknesses are the things which hold us back and prevent us from achieving our goals.

Recognizing our weaknesses and converting them into potential strengths is a way of controlling them. This makes it easier for us to achieve our goals and realize our dreams.

List **some of your weaknesses** below:

For example:

I don't pay attention to detail
I am impatient and impulsive
I don't consider all my options
I tend not to listen sometimes
I sometimes overspend
I sometimes have a high opinion of myself
I tend to do too many things at once
Sometimes I take foolish risks

Sometimes I can be rude and tactless
I can be oversensitive

Tips:

Be honest when answering this question, we all have weaknesses or areas
we can improve
What do others say are areas you can improve on?

My weaknesses are:

Not everyone likes everything about themselves. The good news is that we
have an opportunity to change what we don't like about ourselves. These
dislikes usually hold us back and stop us from moving forward and
progressing with our lives.

List some ways you can overcome the weaknesses you listed above:

Our strengths and weaknesses are our tools and potential tools in
improving our lives. Use them to understand how to best utilize your time.
This could mean developing your strengths further or turning some of your
weaknesses into strengths.

List things you can do to **improve your strengths and reduce your
weaknesses** here:

For example:

Learn to listen to someone else's point of view before making a decision

Learn to plan how to achieve things
Use my computer skills to earn money
Learn to concentrate on one thing at a time
Learn to foresee problems
Make more time for people
Further my computer studies
Try not to be too sensitive
Budget my spending

Tips:

You listed some ways to overcome your weaknesses in the previous section (refer to them when completing the list below).

Consider advice that you received from others in the past that you agree with.

Consider some developmental activities to further develop your strengths and to turn some of your weaknesses into strengths.

Remember your strengths and weaknesses have an important role to play in setting goals for yourself.

List things you can do to **improve your strengths and reduce your weaknesses**:

1.
2.
3.
4.
5.
6.
7.
8.

10 WHAT RESOURCES OR HELP DO I HAVE ACCESS TO?

In order to realize your goals and dreams, you need to know what resources you have available. Resources can be:

Time
Money
Health
Knowledge
Skills
Tools
Help from others
A home office with a computer
Supportive friends who you can count on
Spare time in the evening
A wealth of knowledge about plants and gardening
Shares you can convert into cash

What resources do you have access to?

What skills, knowledge and interests do you have?

How much time, energy and money do you have?

We need to understand that our resources are limited and where we have a shortage in one resource we may be able to top it up by using another resource. For example, if you have plenty of money but not enough time, then you could pay someone to do one of your time consuming tasks.

11 WHAT MAKES ME HAPPY?

"What makes us happy" can be difficult to define because different things make different people happy at different times.

Rather than determining what makes you happy, try to determine when you felt the most content and then determine the elements that helped you to feel that way.

Finding the elements that allowed that general mood of contentment and determining the environment in which you felt that way are the beginning of realizing what makes you happy.

Think about when you were the most happy, and why.

As I said, being "happy" means different things to different people. "Happiness" could mean being at peace, satisfied, carefree or grateful.

To experience happiness you need to undergo "a positive transition". A positive transition is when you go from a low state of being to a higher state of being. For example, by getting a job (that is, going from unemployment to employment) you experience a positive transition and therefore happiness. Other examples of positive transitions are:

Overcoming a sickness
Getting a promotion
Going on holidays
Winning the lotto
Getting married or engaged
Winning a sporting event

A "negative transition" is when you go from a high state of being to a lower state of being. For example, by losing your job (that is, going from employment to unemployment) you experience a negative transition.

Your life can be broken down into 5 areas where you can strive to achieve positive transitions.

These are Spiritual, Mental, Physical, Social and Financial.

Efficient people apply themselves in these 5 areas each and every day. They are sometimes referred to as people who live a "balanced" life.

To experience continual happiness, you need to live a balanced life and undergo positive transitions.

This is the best state that can be achieved, simply because humans always want more and are only temporarily satisfied.

No sooner is one goal achieved (happiness reached) than another one is set because the happiness level from the previous achievement has now been devalued or, should I say, taken for granted. Therefore, the aggregation of short-term happiness is the best one can strive for.

The formula for happiness is to lead a balanced life and strive for positive transitions in each area of your life. The best way to achieve this is by creating your very own personal vision statement, preparing a plan to live that vision and taking action. Remember without action nothing changes.

Now, we all enjoy doing things that make us happy. It makes sense to do these activities more often.

Once you have completed the list below, put these activities into your weekly timetable and start doing them NOW!

Remember, doing things we enjoy more often will make us feel happy more often.

List the things or activities that make you **happy**:

For example:

I enjoy sailing

I enjoy reading
Playing my piano and singing makes me feel good
I like cooking and eating Italian food
Spending time with my family is comforting
I love going on holidays overseas
I like eating out
I like sleeping in on weekends
I like gardening
I enjoy listening to music when exercising

Tips:

"The best time of my life was when I was... (Doing what?)"

"At present I most enjoy..."

What do you enjoy doing in your spare time?

What do you do that fulfils you all the time?

When do you feel like what you're doing is most meaningful?

When did you last say to yourself, "Now that's a job well done," and feel really good about it?

List the things or activities that make you **happy**:

12 SIX CORE HUMAN NEEDS

American life coach, Tony Robbins says that human beings are driven by 6 core needs. These are:

Certainty – the need to be safe, secure, stable, comfortable, predictable, in control, order, remaining in the comfort zone, doesn't try new things, thinks "stay as is". For example, people who do the same things over and over.

Variety – the need for change, uncertainty, surprise, adventure, challenge, risk taking, play, creativity, expressing yourself, thinks "go for it". For example, people who do extreme sports.

Significance – the need to be recognized, to feel important, unique, being different, ego, status, position, proving yourself, getting results, power, thinks "I" or "me". For example, someone who buys a fancy car to show off and stand out so they can satisfy their need for significance.

Love & Connection – the need for bonding, relationship, being part of a community, being like others, conforming, intimacy, sharing yourself, loving others, thinks "you", "we" or "us". For example, a mother caring for her children.

Growth – the need to improve oneself, personal development, learning something new, being better. For example, an athlete trying to get to the top of their sport.

MARTIN FORMATO

Contribution – the need to help others, to serve others, to care, to give and make the world a better place. For example, Mother Teresa.

The first 4 needs are needs of the personality; the last 2 needs are spiritual needs.

To be happy you must satisfy all these needs in a balanced way.

This is easier said than done because some of these needs are opposites. For example, "certainty" is opposite to "variety" and "significance" is opposite to "love and connection".

Someone who is driven by certainty may feel uncomfortable when variety enters his/her life. Someone who is driven by significance may find it difficult to show love and connection.

If you are driven by certainty you may find your life somewhat boring as everything is predictable. Therefore, to spice and balance things up, you will need to add some variety. For example, you could go on a holiday or try something new.

If you are driven by significance then you may find yourself somewhat lonely. Therefore, to balance things up, you could make an effort to get to know people on a personal level.

In general, people driven by the same need tend to get on better. That is, people who are driven by certainty usually get on with people who also are driven by certainty. People who are driven by variety prefer to hang out with other people driven by variety.

The need for growth and contribution is necessary to satisfying your spiritual needs. As you know, you feel good when you are growing as an individual by learning new things and when you help others.

Overall, you should balance your time and energy throughout these 6 needs. Doing this will improve your overall happiness.

Before we leave this topic, please write down the 2 needs which are your dominant needs, out of the 6 core needs:

1.
2.

13 MY VALUES

"Man lives by values; all his enterprises and activities... make sense only in terms of some structure of purposes which are themselves values in action."

Will Herberg

Values are customs we feel strongly about; things that are important to us or things that lead us to ways of acting that seem morally acceptable or desirable.

They generally come from experiences we have had at home, at school, in the community and with other people.

As we grow older, some of our values may change. Environmental influences, our experiences or simply different priorities can cause these changes. For example, a 5-year-old child will value his birthday more than, say, a 45-year-old man.

Values are who we are. They represent our unique and individual essence, our ultimate and most fulfilling form of expressing and relating. Basically, a value is something we cherish and will fight for.

Your values are your internal compass, a place where your passion comes from.

We all have different values, beliefs and standards. Our values influence our belief system.

One way to determine your values is by observing how you react to certain situations. Our values influence the way we respond to people and events.

The more you live aligned to your values the more pleasure and less pain you will have and the less health issues.

The values that you embrace are created from a variety of your life experiences and are at the core of your personality playing a large part in unifying your behavior, shaping your choices and guiding you towards particular goals and objectives.

Values motivate people in their daily lives. Commitment to certain values creates energy and freshness, which, in turn, attracts great success, achievement and joy. Marked improvement can be made in an individual's life by committing to the values he/she believes in.

A value can be defined as a belief or a philosophy that holds importance to you as an individual.

Values are your compass, your code of conduct.

Be true to your values. It is natural to live your values and unnatural not to live your values.

Two values that matter the most to me are:

Myself – I need to take care of both my mental and physical health, so I can help myself and others. If I am not well I cannot help others. I like to eat well, exercise, do interesting work, play and rest. Also to be a good role model for others.

My Relationships – with myself, my creator, my parents, my wife, my children, my extended family, my friends and my community.

Other examples of values are:

Adventure
Achievement
Creativity
Challenge
Community
Dedication
Dignity
Eating well
Enjoyment
Exercise
Family
Financial security
Freedom
Friends
Fulfillment
Fun
Hard work
Health
Honesty
Integrity
Interesting work
Knowledge
Love
Mental health
Money
Myself
Physical health
Play
Power
Recognition
Relationships
Respect
Rest
Self development
Serving others
Team spirit
Trust
Work

Consider people who inspire you or who have had the greatest impact on your life. For them to inspire you or impact you, chances are they have similar values to yourself. List these people and their values.

Who are they?

What do they value?

From the list of values above, or any others you can think of, pick 5 that are important to you and write them below.

Consider values which serve as a guide to the way you behave.

For example: Health, Family, Freedom, Fun and Money

My top 5 values are:

Now let's prioritize your values. By prioritizing your values it will help you make decisions. For example, if you had "family" as a value above "work", then if there was a clash in your time schedule you would choose "family" over "work".

Which one would you consider your most important (number 1)? Write it below together with numbers 2 to 5.

1.
2.
3.
4.
5.

14 CONCLUSION

Thank you again for buying this book!

I hope this book was able to help you discover yourself.

I appreciate you for taking the time out of your day or evening to read this book, and if you have an extra second, I would love to hear what you think about this book or answer any questions.

Please shoot me an email at martin@martinformato.com . I read each and every single email!

I hope you have enjoyed this book as much as I loved writing it for you.

If you enjoyed this book, then I would like to ask you a favor. Would you be kind enough to leave a review for this book on Amazon? I would greatly appreciate it!

Go here: http://amzn.to/2kR4E31

Also if you liked and got value from my book and want more tips on how to Create a Life You Love then please like and subscribe to my other channels below.

Facebook: http://www.facebook.com/doingworkthatmatters

Twitter: http://twitter.com/WorkThatMatter

Instagram: http://www.instagram.com/doing_work_that_matters

Amazon Kindle Books: http://www.amazon.com/Martin-Formato/e/B00M45LI3W

Youtube: https://www.youtube.com/channel/UC_ehfAiip7cBUo-bSdm2uDw

Hopefully by now you feel excited and passionate about your future.

If you liked my writing style, you would absolutely love my new book, **"Follow Your Own Path"**.

This is the coolest book I have ever been involved in and by purchasing a copy you put another copy into the hands of someone less fortunate and you also help me with my mission which is to inspire people to do what they love that also contributes to humanity. That is a win/win/win.

Who Is This Book For?

This book is for anyone who is hungry.
Anyone who wants more out of life.
Anyone who knows that they have more to give, share and experience.
Anyone who feels deep down, in their heart, that they are here for a reason.

It's a book for people who feel stuck, lost, depressed or even suicidal.

In particular, it's for, entrepreneurs who are struggling, school leavers who are lost, employees who are bored or in a job they hate and redundees who feel discarded.

Today, more than ever in history, people need more direction and less information.

This book will put you on the right path, YOUR PATH.

Who Is This Book NOT For?

You should not get this book until you are certain that you truly wish to change your life and you are 100 percent committed to it.

Ask yourself these 2 questions:

Do I want to make a change voluntarily, completely of my own choice?
Do I really want to change my life?

If you cannot honestly say "Yes" without hesitation to both questions, then it is better that you wait until you are serious about changing your life.

As one monk famously said "We want only warriors... victims need not apply".

Go here to get your copy of "Follow Your Own Path"

http://amzn.to/2kQC9CK

If the links do not work, for whatever reason, you can simply search for the title "Follow Your Own Path" on the Amazon website.

Thank you again, and I wish you nothing less than a life you love!

Martin Formato

Email: martin@martinformato.com
Website: www.martinformato.com

Contents from my book "Follow Your Own Path"

What Is This Book About?
Welcome
Introduction
Who Is Martin Formato?
What Is Success?
3 Simple Steps To True Happiness
STEP 1: FIND YOUR PASSION
Success Mindset
The Beginning And The End
Our Philosophy
You Are A Gift
Believe In Yourself
Which Road To Take
Where Do You Want To Go?
Why Do You Want To Go There?
What Makes You Happy?
You Deserve To Be Happy
What Are Your Superpowers?
What Are Your Values?
Success Formula
What's Your Passion Or Purpose?
Your Personal Vision Statement
STEP 2: DEVELOP YOUR PASSION
Where Are You Now?
Challenges And Obstacles
Re-energize and Inspire
Eliminate Excuses
Your Beliefs
How To Change Your Beliefs
Cognitive Behavioral Approach
Balance Is Important
Comfort Zone Danger
What Resources Do You Have Access To?
Develop Your Passion
Who Are Your Role Models?
Who Is Your Ideal Client?
Who Do You Need To Become?
Morning Ritual
Evening Ritual
Thankful List

STEP 3: GIVE YOUR PASSION TO THE WORLD

To get my book go to http://amzn.to/2kQC9CK

If the links do not work, for whatever reason, you can simply search for the title "Follow Your Own Path" on the Amazon website.

15 BONUS FREE BOOK

Go to my website at www.martinformato.com and enter your email address to get my FREE book **"Find Your Gift, Passion and Purpose"**.

Once you register you will be sent FREE information that will further help you create a life you love.

All you have to do is enter your email address to get instant access.

This information will help you get more out of your life — to be able to reach your goals, have more motivation, be at your best, and live the life you have always dreamed of.

I am continually adding new resources, which you will be notified of as a subscriber. These will help you live your life to the fullest!

To get instant access to these incredible tools and resources go to www.martinformato.com

16 ABOUT THE AUTHOR

Hi, I'm Martin Formato, a professional certified life and business coach, motivational speaker and author of the self-help book, "Follow Your Own Path".

My passion is to inspire you to do what you love that also contributes to humanity. How? By helping you express yourself through your passion.

This process will inevitably result in you creating a life you love.

How would you like to jump out of bed every Monday morning, full of excitement about the day ahead because you a living your life with passion and purpose?

I believe that you are a gift to the world and have a passion, gift, talent, skill or ability of some sort, which, once discovered and developed, will open up a whole new, amazing and wonderful world.

What you can contribute no-one else can contribute, because you are unique.

I want to help you find your passion and develop it so you can give it to the world. Why? Because:

I get a buzz helping people transform their life,

The world needs that special something that only you can give,

You deserve to be happy and when you express yourself through your passion you will be happy,

You will love what you do every day and who you are becoming and in the process

You will create a life you love.

By living your passion, you will also be setting an example for your family and friends to do the same. You will inspire them to also go after their dream.

I imagine a world where most people love Mondays because they love what they do; they express themselves through their passion, they help others and fulfill their dream. It doesn't get any better than that!

My blog at www.martinformato.com is my way of sharing ideas, concepts and principles that I have learnt over the last 50 years, which, if acted upon, will allow you to create a life you love. I am sharing this information as my way of giving back to society.

I am thankful to all those men, women and children that I have met throughout my life; some still living and others deceased; the authors of numerous books I have read; seminars I attended; movies and videos I have watched; audios I have listened to; and especially my parents, sister and brothers, my wife, children and relatives for teaching and helping me to shape the person I have become.

It does not matter if you are struggling or doing well, I guarantee that you will learn something from my blog that will make your life better.

My passion is to inspire people to do what they love that also contributes to humanity; to help people create a life they love; to help people find their passion, develop it and give it to the world.

I imagine a world in which everyone loves Mondays because they love what they do and, more importantly, they are proud of whom they have become.

I invite you to be part of our community of people who live passionately, express ourselves and strive to make this a better world.

I am truly thankful for the life I live. I love learning and sharing what I learn so others can benefit. I believe the meaning of life is to grow as an individual so you can help others. To be like a fruit tree that grows and bears fruit for others. That is the secret to a happy life.

Thank you for taking the time to read my message.

Wishing you a life you love!

Martin Formato

PS. If at any point you have any questions, please do not hesitate to contact me. You can best reach me on my blog at www.martinformato.com or simply email me at martin@martinformato.com . Even if you do not have any questions, I would love for you to come by and say hello!

Printed in Great Britain
by Amazon